"The beautiful thing about Gaynor's poems is the **surprise** that is waiting around every corner. The first few lines can start a lump forming in your throat, then the last line provokes a **laugh** escaping without warning. These poems are the kind that you find yourself thinking of, enough to bring you back to them after being out and about and noticing something, some person, some piece of litter, or shadow hitting a wall that makes you think "I **wonder** what James Gaynor would make of that..."

— ANNIE O'NEIL

Director and Producer, *Phil's Camino*
Co-producer and Pilgrim, *Walking the Camino:
Six Ways to Santiago*
Author of *Everyday Camino with Annie*

Everything Becomes a POEM

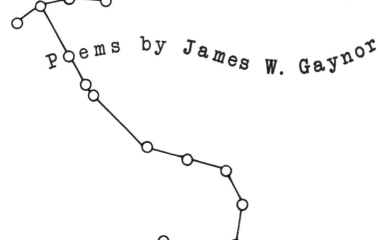

Poems by James W. Gaynor

For
Moses Robert Darche

"Of many Moseses you are my first"

www.facebook.com/NemetonPress
NemetonPress@gmail.com
240 East 76 Street, 15W, New York, NY 10021

ISBN 978-0-9978428-0-7 (paperback)
ISBN 978-0-9978428-1-4 (hardcover)
First Edition
Designed by: Pak Creative, www.pakcreative.com
Set in: Avenir Light & Another Typewriter
Printed and bound by: IngramSpark

Special Thanks

I am deeply grateful to Team Nemeton, an esoteric collective of talent. Gordon Thomas and Patti Frazee demystified every aspect of what it takes to produce a book. Kelly Duke McKinley created a cover design that brilliantly reflects the essence of my poems and allowed me to see dimensions I hadn't previously recognized. Susannah Greenberg made the entire project come together as only a fellow poet — who is also one of the best book publicists in the business — could.

My longtime editor and friend, Peter M. Stevenson, continues to encourage and support my work. "I wonder what Peter will think of this?" is a question I find myself asking whenever I'm close to finishing anything involving the placement of words on paper and the possibility of publication.

That Dan Curley, John S. Hall, and Marion Stein — all writers whose work I admire —took the time to read *Everything Becomes a Poem* and offer their comments touches me more than I can say. The same holds true for Annie O'Neil, who found time amidst the rigors of promoting her latest film, *Phil's Camino*, to share her thoughts with me about this book.

In 1968, Michael Mott — professor, novelist, poet, and best-selling author (*The Seven Mountains of Thomas Merton*) — read one of my poems and told me he thought I might have some talent. I have included "A Change in the Season" in this collection as belated thanks for that encouragement — until now unacknowledged, but always so deeply appreciated.

Many years ago, my life changed when Nancy Kardon Peters and Samantha Rosenberg Darche decided there was room in their family for that guy across the hall. And now there is my beloved grandson, Moses Robert Darche. His arrival on this planet has inspired me to the moon.

This book is for him. ◉

Foreword

Let's start with the titles of the poems: "The Museum of Hideous Bridesmaid Dresses"; "Mme. Curie's Cookbook"; "Cocktails with Aphrodite"; "About the Porn"; "Poetry and Percocet™"; "The Secret to a Happy Married Life (for Men)"; and "We All Agreed About the Salmon."

Think you're in for a bit of fun? You're right.

Fun, of course, is relative. James Gaynor's work limns the darkening of our loves and dreams, the unavoidability of "that occasional howling thing." Endurance in the face of loss, the necessary disillusionment that comes before matured acceptance, the courage to resist familiar demons, and the scruffy joy to be found in friends and dogs — Gaynor's work provokes and consoles in equal measure. ("Never catch a falling knife / Kitchen wisdom from my mother / Who didn't like to cook / But who understood / Danger")

Under Gaynor's scrutiny, big topics such as history, literature, religion, Greek myths, erotic love, and art reveal themselves most intensely in our seemingly mundane moments: an exchange in the dog park, a ride on a city bus, a broken shoelace. His work reminds us that it is often what catches the corner of our eye that deserves prolonged attentiveness. ("I watch her watching / The first firefly she's seen. / Clover-scented night.")

It's worth noting that several of these are New York poems. Not the Arcadian Brooklyn of today, but the gritty, sleepless, and enchanted Manhattan of the 70s, 80s and 90s (e.g., "My friend and neighbor / The Druid priestess / Went to the reading / Without me"). Gaynor writes as wry and grateful survivor, the appreciation for what's been lost never clouding his love for what remains. Read carefully, and you will discern life lessons woven through Gaynor's poetry, suggestions on how to inhabit the world without doing too much damage to oneself and others, and what it might mean to live a long and happy life in our addled 21st Century. And always, throughout these poems, there are eruptions of laughter in the dark. ("After considerable consultation / We have decided / The cat / Will miss you the most.")

With this stunning volume, we find ourselves in the hands of a supremely accomplished poet. The poems are as fine as any I know, and are astonishing for their virtuosity, control, and generosity. If I were to attempt to crystalize James Gaynor's droll and compassionate understanding of our human condition, I'd look to the renowned last lines of Samuel Beckett's 1953 novel, *The Unnamable:* "I can't go on. I'll go on."

Now turn the page. Go on. ◉

....

PETER M. STEVENSON has worked as an editor at *Men's Journal, The New Republic, The New York Observer,* and *Condé Nast Traveler.* A noted journalist and critic, his work appears in many national publications, including *The New Yorker, Esquire,* and *The New York Times.*

Contents

That Thing No One Will Tell You

[For Daniel Evan Lawrence]

Like the silence of a noontime shadow
We all have that thing
No one will tell you

Not your best friend
Not your spouse
Certainly not your absented children

There are variations on the theme
According to season
According to time of day

The unheard music
At 20 is somewhat different
Than the secret at 40

And in darkening life
People can't be bothered
But they don't forget

Like the silence of a noontime shadow
We all have that thing
No one will tell you ◉

Just Another Small Town

mir·a·cle /'mir k( )l/ : *a surprising and welcome event that is not explicable by natural or scientific laws and is therefore considered to be the work of a divine agency.*

Without the tourist attraction
Lourdes is just
Another small town
An ordinary person
With boring shoes
Walking down the street
Hoping
Hoping for a miracle ◎

Changing the Locks

[For Maddy Borak Sylvan]

(As)
It turns out
Marriage was never
In the cards

(Although)
Identical key rings
Were selected
And exchanged

(So)
When everything ended
The locksmith
Was called

(Because)
It's not official
Until
The locks are changed

(And)
Then it is
But only when it's over
As it turns out ◎

On Paper

[For Anne Gaynor]

We are always
Smiling
In photographs.

Making me wonder —

What we were thinking,
Really.

Many (almost all) these
Shows of teeth
Foreshadowed present grief.

Starting with the hair —

Really,
What were we thinking? ◎

New York Evening: Three Haiku

1.

I watch her watching
The first firefly she's seen.
Clover-scented night.

2.

Five-hundred-year-old
Laughter in summer darkness.
Shakespeare in the Park.

3.

Watch out! But I saw
Only the pointing finger,
Not the speeding car. ◉

Epithalamium

Every marriage is a first
Not so each wedding
Yours are now reunions
Aging acquaintances
Taking attendance
(And we lie about how good we look)

(April 17, 1971)
City Hall
About which
Less said the better
Though your father
Kept finding words
(And we still wonder what happened to the groom)

(June 21, 1976)
Bridesmaids and ushers
Your parents were pleased
The food was excellent
But the dress wore you
An omen disregarded in all the froth
(And we're divided on the issue of his parole)

(October 22, 1993)
A pre-nup
Beige and ivory
A better fit
Though his children's behavior
Set off a few alarms
(And we remember what you said at the funeral)

(January 31, 2015)
Another plunge
This time pastel
Two sets of grandchildren
Optimism triumphal
Experience mute
(And we agree about good deals on used cars) ◉

Meeting Moses

[For Moses Robert Darche]

Of many Moseses
You are
My first

And not only in your name
Is there a
Promised Land

(That place
We will not know
Together)

But also in your
Clear gray gaze
A wordless poem

The beginning of our journey
Each a grand person
In the other's eyes ◉

That Occasional Howling Thing

(Wednesday, 3 a.m.)
City silence
Is selective
Sirens
Cars
That occasional howling thing

(Sunday, midnight)
Country quiet
Is frantic
Crickets
Owls
That occasional howling thing

(24/7)
White noise
Is constant
Everyone not saying what they
Really think about your spouse
That occasional howling thing ◉

It Takes the Time It Takes

[For Tim Kittleson]

In a classic French novel
Unopened for years
A snapshot / bookmark
Marks the place we were

As you and I surface in her story
The princess ponders
The duke may well have other motives
Her husband is not pleased

There are figures in the distance
Just as we are likely
Background in someone else's
Memory from a waning afternoon

It takes the time it takes
Creased
Faded
We are now the picture. ◉

(The Edge of Madness Is)

[For Liza Morse]

(The edge of madness is)
Not the cliff
Off which you plunge
Or where you dance
To dramatic background music

(The edge of madness is)
A country without borders
A paper cut
A sudden sinkhole in the linoleum
The cat underfoot

(The edge of madness is)
The old man at the museum
 Wearing shorts
And hiking boots
Talking to the Vermeer

(The edge of madness is)
Hiding in unmapped details
Lurking at the curb
Just one mismatched pair of socks
Away   ◉

The Grief of Small Things Breaking

It is not only
A shoelace
But also the grief
Of small things breaking

Together
We bought the shoes
They went with the suit
The ties
The bold striped socks
I wore them
In an office life
Which
Like the suit
No longer fits
And when we danced
Together

It is not only
A shoelace
But also the grief
Of small things breaking ◉

In Lieu of Flowers
(The New York Times, 16 August 2015)

1. Younger

Suddenly / Deep sadness / Broken hearts, sense of loss /
Generous, kind, self-effacing / Survived by

Suddenly, with deep sadness,
Loss is sensed.

Generous, kind, self-effacing —
They are
Broken-heartedly survived.

2. The Same Age

Remarkable, beautiful, vivacious / Companion / Educated at /
Loving, kind / Will be missed / Leaves behind

Not to speak ill of the dead,
But
Were they really
Remarkable, beautiful and vivacious?

No matter.

They had companions and
Were educated —
Always passively —
At institutions worthy of mention.
Loving and kind,
They will be missed
By those they leave behind.

3. Older

Pioneer / Self-made / End of an era / Treasured /
Donations in memory of / Beloved, cherished devoted /
Mourn the passing / Longtime partner / Preceded in death /
In lieu of flowers

Self-made people!
Inevitably, they mark the
End of an era (theirs).

Treasured, they are
Worthy
Of donations
Made in their memory.

A beloved, cherished, devoted crowd
Mourns their passing, as do
Longtime partners.

Pioneers they may have been,
But it appears that they are often
Preceded in death.

And as a final request,
They would very much appreciate
Something,
A gesture,
More substantial than flowers. ◉

Never Catch a Falling Knife

[For Michaela Cassidy]

Never catch a falling knife

Kitchen wisdom from my mother
Who didn't like to cook
But who understood
Danger

In shadows of a Florida evening
Rathers emerged
Hers a business
A travel agency with her name

That overarching rather
Always present in the kitchen
But good to hear
And good to know

Never catch a falling knife ◉

Time / Space

They are wrong
Who say
Time
Is the great healer
He isn't

Space
Creates her double distance
Holding us gently
Rocking
Rocking ◎

Destiny in Midtown

I seem to have misplaced my destiny
In the search for love,
Five fewer pounds,
Better glass frames.

Or perhaps my destiny has misplaced me,
While books go unwritten,
Music never heard,
Injustice not addressed.

Meanwhile,
I walk the dog,
Shop for food,
Do the laundry.

And here's the downtown bus —
I am running,
Per usual,
About five minutes late. ◉

We All Agreed About the Salmon

We could not know then
How it would play out,
But
We all agreed about the salmon.

Time wavered.
Promises and speeches made,
There was dancing.

We went home,
Not knowing,
But
We all agreed about the salmon. ◎

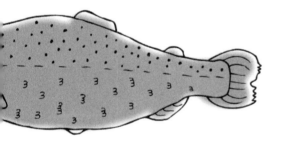

In the Closet that Is Memory

Absent friends
Still claim their space
In the closet that is memory

They are the clothes
We keep hoping will
Come back

Into style
Or at the very least
Fit us again

As once
Perhaps (only perhaps)
They did so well

As once
We thought
They did so well ◎

Subway Aria

We are standing still,
Moving.
Pressed close enough

To pretend
We are not here.
In silent agreement
We do not see each other.

I do not envy your single rose.
You do not wonder who
Still wears a wristwatch.

We are standing still,
Moving.
Same car.
Same train.
Different destinations. ◉

In Dog Years

[For Judith Hendra]

He sits
In the afternoon sun
With
His milky-eyed
Once-a-wolf

Same bench
Same time
Each day
They
Compete

Neck and neck
Racing
Against
Each other
Both knowing

Winner
And / or
Loser
She is his
Final dog ◎

The Last Word

Each family is a work of fiction
This one, not so much a tree
As flowering vine
Twisting through the garden
Strangling everything
Growing in its path.

Case in point: Great-aunt Louisine [not her real name]
Her British poet lover mourned her as
A sunny tower room in winter —
Sweeping vistas,
But chilly.
Her younger sister said she was a plate of tainted soup.

A terrifying first husband, then an expensive Italian prince
She was known to kick the occasional dog or child.
Famous for her hats
And popular in Paris,
Louisine [not her real name] appeared in poems, portraits
And a roman à clef about lesbians on a Greek island.

Still a subject of discussion,
Two museums and three Spanish great-grandchildren
Continue to fight about the paintings,
While upkeep of the French mausoleum
Creates polite Christmas disagreement
Among the American cousins.

She left everything to the chauffeur
Louisine [not her real name] was not an easy person to love.
Far from it, according to our grandmother (her younger sister),
Herself a subject of neither literature nor painting,
But who always had
The last word. ◉

Notes on Condolence

Of little comfort to know:
    Our dear — a few not quite so — departed
    Are living
    Not always as the happiest of roommates
    In our thoughts

Even less reassuring to think:
    Our dear — a few not quite so — departed
    Are waiting
    Not always patiently
    For it to be our turn to leave

Colder still to grasp:
    Then — only then — when
    We are finally locked in other peoples' memories
    All our dear — a few not quite so — departed
    Can move on

Important to remember:
    On occasions requiring condolence
    Promise faithfully
    To keep the living in our thoughts
    Forget the dead immediately ◎

Ave Atque Vale

After considerable consultation
We have decided
The cat
Will miss you the most.

Everyone else
(Including the dog)
Views your departure
With mixed feelings.

(Particularly the dog) ◎

Lost in [the] Translation

*Et dès que j'eus reconnu le goût du morceau de madeleine
trempé dans le tilleul que me donnait ma tante (quoique
je ne susse pas encore et dusse remettre à bien plus tard
de découvrir pourquoi ce souvenir me rendait si heureux),
aussitôt la vieille maison grise sur la rue, où était sa chambre,
vint comme un décor de théâtre s'appliquer au petit pavillon,
donnant sur le jardin, qu'on avait construit pour mes parents
sur ses derrières (ce pan tronqué que seul j'avais revu
jusque-là); et avec la maison, la ville, la Place où on
m'envoyait avant déjeuner, les rues où j'allais faire des
courses depuis le matin jusqu'au soir et par tous les temps,
les chemins qu'on prenait si le temps était beau.*

The taste —
A dissolving, tea-soaked cookie
 Melted his thoughts
A kaleidoscope of what was no more —
His rustic, bed-living aunt
    (tilleul-brewing Léonie),
Hier old, gray house
    (a stage of sorts),
 Single-steepled Combray
    (meandering country-byways).

He did not know
Then
Why
He was so happy
To drink tea
And remember. ◉

Sequels: Life and Art

[For Dan Curley]

We now understand
It did not end

The first time
Was an installment

Sequels in film
Sequels in life

But second honeymoons
Rarely recreate

The suspension of disbelief
So necessary to the first ◎

My Last Boyfriend
*(After Robert Browning)**

LOS ANGELES

That's my last boyfriend hanging on the wall
Looking as if he were alive. Worth all
I paid the artist. Yes, that painter, noted
Catamite to an author devoted
To tales of lovesick men. Stand there. Feel free
To ask. That lidded glance, half-smile, how he
Captured — just so — that invitation you
Now read. Contrapposto in Malibu.
What caused that burning look? His knowing glance?
I was not alone gliding in the dance.
There was the artist and a man outside —
Tan, bare-chested, spraying insecticide
The painter may have prayed to do justice
To his abs, or praised the hairless crevice
Between his pecs. Whatever. The boy had
A groin — how shall I say? — too soon made glad,
Too easily impressed. He liked all he
Looked at, and his looks traveled globally.
No difference — my presence in our bed,
A well-packed Speedo on the beach observed —
All birthed that lazy smirk. As if to rate
My billion-dollar heft equal in weight
To anyone whose blue-jeaned buttocks he,
In trademark innocence, found grin-worthy.
Perhaps I should have deigned to talk, to peel
Away what didn't work. But I don't kneel
To anyone. Oh, yes, he smiled, no doubt,

* *My Last Duchess* by Robert Browning (see page 70)

Each time we met but who else came without
Much the same smile? I knew. I gave commands.
Then all smiles stopped together. There he stands
As if alive. So. Let's go down and meet
The guests. Your agency is most discreet;
My lawyer has the non-disclosure forms.
The silkscreen on your left, a can of worms —
Unusual in Pop Art History —
Which Warhol numbered and then signed for me! ◎

Five Stages of Death in the Morning

The ritual begins
The night before
When the body is committed
To the bed
In sure and certain hope
Of resurrection
In the morning

Waking to
An alarm clock-based liturgy of
Denial
Anger
Bargaining
Depression
Acceptance

Again and again
Five stages of death
In the morning
Sure and certain
Until the inevitable
But let's not go there
Just yet ◎

The Nightly News

For people who know each other only
By their dogs' names and
For those who read a

Scent-based alphabet
The rusting corner lamppost is
Where and how both groups catch up

Lexington's dad is getting divorced
Due (in part) to his affair with Davidson's person
Mazurka ate the tutu

Her guys thought would be
Such fun for Halloween
And everyone hates the Shar Pei ◎

Street Smarts
[For Annie O'Neil]

Pre ear buds and blue teeth
It was easy
To know who was crazy
And who was not
On the sidewalk

No longer

Where once the person
Talking animatedly to the air was to be
Stepped around
Ignored
And evaluated as a reason to cross the street

Today

That vocalizing person
Could just as easily be
Launching an IPO or
Breaking up with a boyfriend as
Arguing with a dead grandmother

Back to basics

A distant voice (my mother's?)
From Urban Survival 101:
"Always look at the shoes.
Crazy people wear
Crazy shoes." ◉

What to Tell You When You Wake

I watch and listen as you sleep
Tomorrow
Someone
Will point out
Life goes on
Which
Of course
It does
With interruptions
But what to tell you when you wake? ◉

The Museum of Hideous Bridesmaid Dresses

The museum is a popular
Weekend tourist destination
Currently featuring:
"Chiffon and Sun Tzu's *The Art of War.*"

Military action is the path
Of life and death for every nation
And worthy of study.
    — "Strategic Assessments"

The entry fee includes a guided tour
Led by a lieutenant colonel (ret.)
Who most recently
Occupied Iraq.

Destroy the energy
Of the enemy's armies
By killing their generals' hearts.
    — "Armed Struggle"

This collection proves
In sickness and in health
No one ever looked good
Wearing orange.

Those who triumph
Without fighting
Are the true champions.
    — "Planning a Siege"

A designer explosion in violent green
Demonstrates how bankrupting one's attendants
Is an effective way
To maintain control.

The most important characteristic
Of any military action
Is not persistence but victory.
 — *"Doing Battle"*

In this building
White
Does not signal
Surrender.

About the Porn
[For John Jack Hall]

If you're reading this
You've opened the box and
Now have met
Those special friends about whom
I never talked.

Think of them (please) as
Unconventionally dressed mourners
You'll be spared at the
Funeral and the
Reading of the will.

Although there are a
Few favorites who
Deserve some recognition for
All their years of
Faithful service. ◎

No, Not Yet

The singer
Hears it
She tells herself
No, not yet

The model
Sees it
He tells himself
No, not yet

Voices crack
Buttocks sag
We tell ourselves
No, not yet ◉

Usually an Aunt

(If)
A family can be
Metaphored as
Complicated geography with
Singular customs and
An undocumented language

(Then)
Someone
Usually an aunt
Is the connecting river that
Spines the country and
Regulates trade

(But)
Borders shift
Cities vanish
Rivers change course
Leaving behind a few artifacts and
Some fading maps   ◎

Cocktails with Aphrodite

In any war
The side she backs
Loses.

Every morning she awakes,
Virgo intacta,
Having learned nothing from the night before.

Laughter-loving, she is the least intelligent
Of all the gods and of their jokes
The divine butt.

Popular at parties, she arrives
Mist-wrapped, at least an hour late
And all heads turn. Conversation stops.

While across that crowded, silent room,
Pallas Athena and ox-eyed Hera
Glower vengefully, plotting. ◉

Daily Horoscopes of the Gods Deciphered: 12 Cautionary Haikus

Hera (Aquarius): "You may feel somewhat neglected and unappreciated."

Beware the affair
With a husband not your own.
Mrs. Zeus hates that.

Ares (Scorpio): "You could start to feel a bit unsatisfied with the status quo."

Boredom often leads
To small wars between nations
With oddly spelled names.

Aphrodite (Taurus): "A new love interest appears."

The heart may always
Have its reasons. But, really,
You should know better.

Hermes (Cancer): "Lines of communications might get crossed."

Nothing to do when
Mercury dances retro.
Blame the stars and wait.

Athena (Aries): "You have a tendency to overthink things."

Zeus had a headache
From his daughter's OCD.
There was no aspirin.

Poseidon (Pisces): "Be aware of possible boundary issues."

Pre the tsunami
A trip to the beach seemed like
Such a good idea.

Demeter (Virgo): "You would benefit by spending more time with family."

Unanswered phone calls
To Persephone result
In global warming.

Hephaistos (Libra): "You may be using work as a means of escape."

His workshop is a
Volcano far, far
Away from his wife.

Hestia (Capricorn): "You need to get out of the house more."

Face it. Something's wrong
When every Christmas you get
A vacuum cleaner.

Apollo (Gemini): "A new relationship requires subtle charm."

Daphne snarled, "Get lost,
You old lech! I'll scream!!" And then
She became a tree.

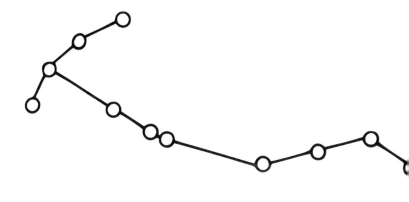

Artemis (Sagittarius): "An unintended encounter could have unexpected results."

Acteon should know.
Chance meetings with Artemis —
Not a good idea.

Zeus (Leo): "Too much focus on your career could cause unhappiness at home."

The unpleasantness
At Troy directly followed
Thunder on the Mount. ◉

The Boardroom in the Park

Not unlike
Mahogany and chrome-polished
Corporate chambers

The neighborhood dog run
Is a regular destination
With familiar protocols

Cautious greeting precedes
Ritual butt-sniffing
To determine the alpha

And in ending our gatherings
Even if we accomplished
Nothing else

We know
Who's on top
Today ◉

Joe [Heart Emoticon] Mary

[For Patricia Wiley]

Among the characters in the
Midnight at the stable
Fa la la
Cherubim in the rafters
Scenario
Joe has always been
My favorite

But Mary's story of
How it all came about
Must have been
Difficult to swallow
Even if Joe
Believed
In angels

It seems more likely
Her parents
Anxious to
Avoid scandal
Offered to
Set him up in his own
Carpentry shop

Whatever
Happened or didn't
When I see a crèche
I like to think
Joe [heart emoticon] Mary
On the way to Bethlehem
He held her and said

We'll work it out
If it's a girl
I hope she'll be just like you
And if a boy
I'll teach him how to work with wood
No matter what
We'll be a family ◎

Musical Chairs

The crystal-ball custom known as
Musical Chairs
Foretells future success via a
Diminishing arrangement of furniture

The game mirrors Life (with a
Capital L)
Where strategy intersects with
Orchestrated luck
The winner here is not the last
Child left standing
But the only one sitting when the
Melody ends
Surrounded by chair-less ex-friends
Who find comfort
In cake and now want to blow out
A few candles

And so it continues measuring years
Danced in circles
Musical Chairs in Life (with a
Capital L) ◉

Poetry and Percocet™

[For Anne Gaynor]

My friend and neighbor
The Druid priestess
Went to the reading
Without me
Which was probably just as well

As I was recovering from the loss of a tooth
Couldn't hear out of one ear and occasionally lost my balance
Though I suppose if I had fallen over we could always have
Blamed a contraindicated combination of
Poetry and Percocet™

She met the famous poet
He remembered her from the last time
But who forgets a Druid priestess
And she told him she had given away all his books
As gifts and he said something great will come to you

At that very moment
A woman handed her an extra ticket
And said please give this to someone who needs one
The poet overheard and smiled
See said he

So now I wish that I had gone
And risked a loss of equilibrium
Because we could always have
Blamed a contraindicated combination of
Poetry and Percocet™ ◎

A Change in the Season

[For Michael Mott]

It is spring
I suppose
There are kites in the air
And students
Wearing sweaters
With letters
Everywhere ◎

Migrating Pain

[For Karen Green]

We had been together my lower left canine and I
For more than 50 years but there is
No ceremony to help the aging mourn
The loss of a tooth and there should be because

We shared countless meals and we
Appear together in hundreds of smiling
Photographs but no one seems to understand
The pain which is both real and

Psychological and then it migrated to my left ear and
Now in addition to the open grave in my jaw
I can't hear on that side which has left me thinking
About how did I get here so here goes

It all started when according to my mother
Whose version of history was at times fanciful
Her side left Scotland in 17-something before the
English could kill them settling in upstate New York

Where most of them but not all then died in an
Indian attack and my father's family left Ireland in 1863
Before the English could kill them arriving in New York City
Just in time for the Draft Riots so someone said

Let's lose the O at the beginning of our last name and
Nobody got shot which is how I got here contemplating the
Lack of a consoling ritual to mark the death of a tooth and
How it's all about years and years of migrating pain ◉

The Secret to a Happy Married Life (for Men)

Rather late in the season
I have at last discovered
The secret to a happy
Married life for my gender.

It is based on daily awe,
Gratitude to be the one
Man deemed worthy of serving
A silken doe-eyed goddess.

I'm now that delirious
Bumper sticker of a guy
Who would like to be the dude
He hopes his dog may think him.

And there it has always been,
In plain sight, the key to bliss,
A truth repeated over years:
Life's a bitch. ◎

Her Previous Person

Though we are now
Thoroughly bonded
I was not her
First nor was she mine

And on the street
I often think she
Hopes to find her
Previous person

I cannot know
But imagine as
An old woman
Who died leaving her

Without a lap
Needing someone to
Risk the daily
Past-life regression

Otherwise known
As walking the dog ◎

That Last Time We Were All Together

Among the photographs we insist on keeping
There is always one of what we think was
That last time we were all together raising the questions if

We knew then what we know now
Would we have done things differently or
What would we have said or not said but

It's also a picture of what remains unseen
Not so much a group likeness as a
Map of shifting alliances plus

That last time we were all together
Was actually somewhere else and
Nobody had a camera. ◉

Something About Mayhap
(First known use circa 1531)

Mayhap
Because I have always wanted to be
Someone named Oberon in whose life
The use of mayhap would not be
Unusual
Where forsooth and perchance
Could surface
Without apology or explanation
Along with the occasional
Gadzooks

This last a contraction of
God's hooks
Aka the crucifixion nails
Although why I know that and
Cannot remember
Any of my PINS
Remains mysterious much like
Why I am not called Oberon or
The waning popularity of
Mayhap ◎

Dorothea Restructured

[HT, George Eliot]

*"But the effect of her being on those around her was
incalculably diffusive: for the growing good of the world
is partly dependent on unhistoric acts; and that things
are not so ill with you and me as they might have been,
is half owing to the number who lived faithfully a hidden
life, and rest in unvisited tombs."*

She merited what is
One of the best last lines
Ever because
The effect of her being on
Those around her was
Incalculably diffusive

And Dorothea embodied
Both a trend and a truth
Since the growing good of
The world is
Partly dependent on
Unhistoric acts

Standing firmly in contrast to her sister
Who was fond of geraniums but
Did not particularly care
Whether things are not so ill with
You and me as
They might have been

Dorothea Brooke Casaubon Ladislaw
Lived faithfully a
Life hidden in the environs of
Middlemarch but
She does not rest in
An unvisited tomb ◎

Mme. Curie's Cookbook

Eventually her work would prove deadly
The glowing tubes she liked to carry in her pockets
Whose soft light she found enchanting

Killed her and made her notebooks into
Hazmat so dangerous to read or handle
They are still entombed in lead-lined boxes

Even her cookbook is poisonous meaning
Hidden deep within the millennial half-life of Radium is
Mme. Curie's recipe for mayonnaise ◉

La Traviata for Dummies

[For Jeff Bowles]

Once upon a Belle Époque
In an apartment well beyond her means
On the fashionable rue Gambetta
Lived the beautiful Violetta

Her boyfriend's name was Alfredo
Not even close friends would call him Al
They fell in love though his father objected
Then nothing went quite as expected

Vi was not well and Al not too bright
Their overture was in E major
Everyone knew sadly
It would all end badly

And it did ◎

Oral History

[For Kate Pulley]

According to Kate's mother
Herself
A legend to her daughter's friends
Kate's grandmother
Who was a Baptist teetotaler
Until she discovered wine
Was in no way bothered
When her husband
Played cards with
Lucky Luciano
On the gangster's boat
In Long Beach

According to my mother
Herself
Something of an enigma to all concerned
My grandmother
Who said the rosary daily and
Liked ribbon candy
Was in no way bothered
By her husband who
Wore glasses and
Apparently
Led a blameless life
In Albany

Some people have all the luck ◉

A Poem About a Pigeon

"All I really want to do is paint light on the side of a house."
Edward Hopper

Sometimes
The sheen on a pigeon's feathers
Is only that
Nothing more
Or less

And sometimes
A poem about a pigeon
Is a poem about a pigeon
Nothing more
Or less ◎

Still Lifes

[For Robin Glazer]

A still life (plural still lifes) is a work of art depicting mostly inanimate subject matter, typically commonplace objects which may be either natural (food, flowers, deadanimals,plants,rocks,orshells)orman-made(drinking glasses, books, vases, jewelry, coins, pipes, and so on).

One still life
Safely celebrating the inanimate
Is usually sufficient

                and

There is occasional interest
In identifying the artist rather than
Bothering with yet another bouquet

                but

In the plural
Still lifes
Become problematic

            because

Nothing is more deadly
Both in language and art
Than a collection of still lifes

          although

Their frames
Sometimes retain
A writhing gilded menace

        particularly

In contrast to
All the absence
They surround   ◎

Bedtime Story

[For Susannah Greenberg]

I remember
Voices in the wind
And children who didn't listen
Ended very badly

Sometimes the wind was a tree or
A bird or a spider
The message was always the same
Things happen in the dark

I never heard the voices
Not for lack of listening
The difference being now I know
Things happen in the dark   ◉

Before / After
[For Samantha Rosenberg Darche]

I had of course a suitable amount of time to adjust to the idea
But I'm not sure it could ever
Have been enough since it was only a few years ago
She was riding her pink tricycle and how
Now she is old enough to have career and a husband and a child is
Beyond comprehension and
Probably the subject for something else about time and age
But I digress

Before

I imagined a twig in winter
Gelid sap and frosty air
I would be the transgrandparent
A James Bond version of Auntie Mame
Just in from somewhere not here
Stepping out of a limousine
Jumping off a motorcycle
Immediately identifiable as
The One Not Like The Others
I would discreetly flaunt my
Japanese tattoos and
Mysterious companion
Known only as
Gregg the Surf God with Three Gs

After

What actually happened is
A bunny named Pat
On appointed evenings I trail
A little body who can say
Please / thank you / woof and
Sits in my lap as we read about
A bunny named Pat
The only connection
Between the two grandfathers
Is the sap
Far from hidden deep
In a December branch
It is what
I have become   ◎

Long Story Short

Long story short
I was in a car with
POTUS and
FLOTUS
Laughing and
Eating jelly donuts

Then I woke up
The dog and
The cat were
Curled up next to each other and
That never happens
Swear to god ◉

After All This Time

1. Your Bookcase

Your bookcase is
As you left it
Shelves buckling
Under the weight of your
Inquiring and
Acquisitive mind

Mysteries abound
Among them
Why three copies of
The Last of the Mohicans and
That particular issue of
Foreign Affairs from 1976

All groaning together
In a system that
May have had something
To do with trim size and
Jacket color
But I have no idea

2. The Cat Was Switzerland

The cat was Switzerland
In the war
Your idea
Not mine
A dispassionate observer
Unaffected by the
Treaty negotiations
And cease fires
Surrounding his dish

Since the armistice
He has annexed
Your side of the bed
At night
Which I might
Count as a victory
But due to
My allergies it remains
Pyrrhic at best

3. After All This Time

After all this time
Your side of the closet
Remains empty
What clothes I have
In need of hanging
Still respect
The boundary negotiations
The lasting truce between
Our once-warring countries
After all this time ◎

Moo

[For Moses Robert Darche]

It's always a good idea to get the fact
my grandson is a genius
out of the way early in the conversation
although I have already
provided sufficient examples to prove my case

and should

by now have created an agreed-upon framework
that would save all of us a lot of time but never mind
when asked after being read the book about cows
forming a labor union because the barn is cold and
they want electric blankets you know the one I mean

and if

you don't you should because it too is genius
so anyway when he was asked if he knew
what sound a cow makes
he appeared to give it some thought
Before saying "Yes"

and then

he found something better to do which
turned out to be singing to the dog
leaving all concerned with a sense he might
be destined for the law or possibly preparing
to testify under oath somewhere

and if

he is going to be this sophisticated
or seriously let's face it bordering on
just a bit sarcastic and world-weary for
someone who's not even two yet we'd better
start with the French Existentialists now.

Genius. ◎

Translating Verlaine:
Three Easy Steps

[For Kelly Duke McKinley]

1. Il Pleure Dans Mon Cœur

Il pleure dans mon coeur
Comme il pleut sur la ville;
Quelle est cette langueur
Qui pénètre mon coeur?

Ô bruit doux de la pluie
Par terre et sur les toits!
Pour un coeur qui s'ennuie,
Ô le chant de la pluie!

Il pleure sans raison
Dans ce coeur qui s'écoeure.
Quoi! nulle trahison? ...
Ce deuil est sans raison.

C'est bien la pire peine
De ne savoir pourquoi
Sans amour et sans haine
Mon coeur a tant de peine!

2. My Heart Weeps

My heart weeps.
Like rain falling upon the city;
What is this languid
Piercing sensation?

Sweet sound of the drops
On the ground and roofs!
For a distracted lover,
Oh, there is music in the rain!

My sickened heart
Weeps without reason.
Surprise! There was no betrayal?!
This mourning is senseless.

By far the worst pain
Is not to know why that
Without love, without hate
My heart still fills with anguish!

3. No One Likes a Man Who Cries

Paul, Paul, Paul, Paul,
All that weeping and the weather —
Though high barometric pressure
Has been known to cause depression
In poets and btw

Paul, Paul, Paul, Paul,
Your doomed love of boys
And resulting messy dramas
Now seem merely an excuse for
Water works and btw

Paul, Paul, Paul, Paul,
You weep because it is your nature —
Though all that absinthe
May well have been
A contributing factor. ◉

Everything Becomes a Poem

[For Jenny Rodriguez]

A gray-eyed baby
Goddesses in crowded rooms
Space (her double distance)
Misplaced destinies
Absent friends
And a subway pole
Everything becomes a poem   ◉

Notes

My Last Duchess
Robert Browning (1842)

FERRARA

That's my Last Duchess painted on the wall,
Looking as if she were alive. I call
That piece a wonder, now: Frà Pandolf's hands
Worked busily a day, and there she stands.
Will't please you sit and look at her? I said
"Frà Pandolf" by design, for never read
Strangers like you that pictured countenance,
The depth and passion of its earnest glance,
But to myself they turned (since none puts by
The curtain I have drawn for you, but I)
And seemed as they would ask me, if they durst,
How such a glance came there; so, not the first
Are you to turn and ask thus. Sir, 'twas not
Her husband's presence only, called that spot
Of joy into the Duchess' cheek: perhaps
Frà Pandolf chanced to say "Her mantle laps
Over my lady's wrist too much," or "Paint
Must never hope to reproduce the faint
Half-flush that dies along her throat": such stuff
Was courtesy, she thought, and cause enough
For calling up that spot of joy. She had
A heart—how shall I say?—too soon made glad,
Too easily impressed; she liked whate'er
She looked on, and her looks went everywhere.
Sir, 'twas all one! My favour at her breast,

The dropping of the daylight in the West,
The bough of cherries some officious fool
Broke in the orchard for her, the white mule
She rode with round the terrace—all and each
Would draw from her alike the approving speech,
Or blush, at least. She thanked men,—good! but thanked
Somehow—I know not how—as if she ranked
My gift of a nine-hundred- years-old name
With anybody's gift. Who'd stoop to blame
This sort of trifling? Even had you skill
In speech—(which I have not)—to make your will
Quite clear to such an one, and say, "Just this
Or that in you disgusts me; here you miss,
Or there exceed the mark"—and if she let
Herself be lessoned so, nor plainly set
Her wits to yours, forsooth, and made excuse,
—E'en then would be some stooping; and I choose
Never to stoop. Oh sir, she smiled, no doubt,
Whene'er I passed her; but who passed without
Much the same smile? This grew; I gave commands;
Then all smiles stopped together. There she stands
As if alive. Will't please you rise? We'll meet
The company below, then. I repeat,
The Count your master's known munificence
Is ample warrant that no just pretence
Of mine for dowry will be disallowed;
Though his fair daughter's self, as I avowed
At starting, is my object. Nay, we'll go
Together down, sir. Notice Neptune, though,
Taming a sea-horse, thought a rarity,
Which Claus of Innsbruck cast in bronze for me! ◉

About the Author

James W. Gaynor is a poet, artist, editor, and writer.
A graduate of Kenyon College, he has lived in Paris, where
he taught a course on Emily Dickinson at the University
of Paris, studied the development of the psychological
novel in 17th-century France, and worked as a translator.

After returning to New York, Gaynor worked as an editor at
Grosset & Dunlap, *Cuisine* magazine, *Scriptwriter News* and
Forbes Publications, where he was on the editorial staff of
the *Social Register*. His articles, book reviews and essays have
appeared in *The New York Observer*, and he recently retired
as the Global Verbal Identity Leader for Ernst & Young LLP.

A silver medalist in the 1994 Gay Games (Racewalking),
Gaynor's found-object sculpture has been exhibited internationally.
He is a member of the Advisory Board of New York's The
Creative Center at University Settlement, a nonprofit organization
dedicated to bringing the creative arts to people with cancer
and chronic illnesses (www.thecreativecenter.org)

An avid urbanite, Gaynor lives in New York City. ◉

Photo credit: ROBERT SCHECHTER

CPSIA information can be obtained
at www.ICGtesting.com
Printed in the USA
BVOW11s0142161116

467962BV00004B/8/P

9 780997 842807